THE QUEST FOR GLORY

by Randy Meulman

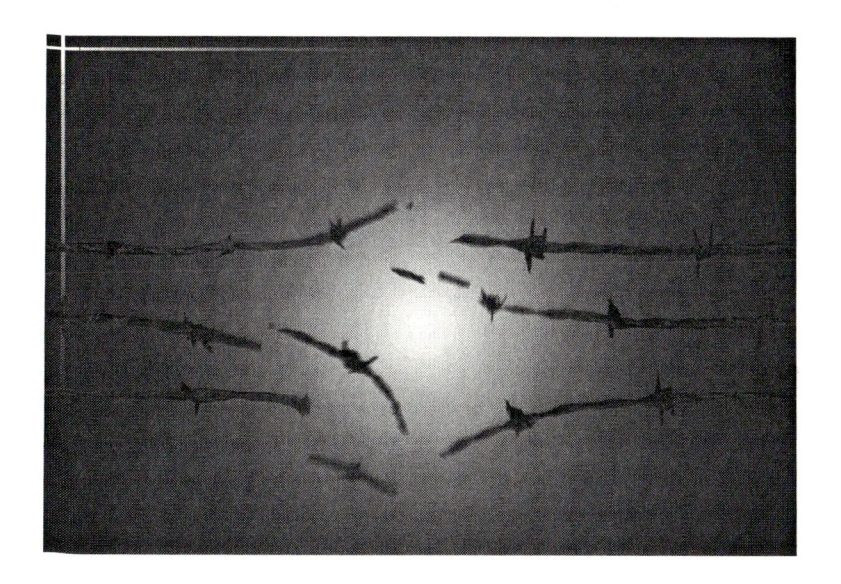

Live in Freedom
Not Fenced in by Legalism

The Quest for Glory
by Randy Meulman

Published by:
John Meulman
Dallas, Texas 75225

ISBN 0-9774730-0-7

This book, *The Quest for Glory*, is available
through booksellers and directly from the publisher.

To contact the publisher send an email:
mailto:publisher@TheQuestForGlory.com

Or go to the Web site for *The Quest for Glory*:
http://www.TheQuestForGlory.com

Copyright © 2005 by **Randy Meulman**

The material in this book, including any electronic version, may be used and copied freely for any educational or personal use. All rights to material in this book, including any electronic version, are retained by copyright holder. The material in this book, including any electronic version, may not be copied or reproduced in any way except as specified in this copyright notice. The material in this book, including any electronic version, may not be used at all for commercial use or for the purpose of receiving profit or remuneration of any kind without the express written consent of the copyright holder.

TABLE OF CONTENTS

GLORY 4

SPECIAL THANKS TO 5

PREFACE 6

Chapter 1:   The Holy Spirit 10

Chapter 2:   The Spirit of Death 13

Chapter 3:   A Miraculous Glimpse behind the Curtain 23

Chapter 4:   The Aftermath 25

Chapter 5:   The Holy Spirit's Purpose 29

Chapter 6:   Religious Abuse 37

Chapter 7:   Born Again 40

Chapter 8:   Born into Freedom—Sold into Slavery 43

Chapter 9:   Looking for a Few Good Men 47

Chapter 10:   My Eternal Break with Religion 52

Chapter 11:   Broken in the Wilderness 55

Chapter 12:   Resurrection 59

Chapter 13:   The Choice 66

GLORY

There is something inside each of us that yearns for more. A starving person can, of course, only think of a morsel of food, and a thirsty one, a cup of water. But, take a person who has been given everything he ever desired, with all of his dreams fulfilled—and you will find that individual searching for more.

I believe at the core of much of our searching lies an aching heart that knows it was created for more. Have you noticed there is a "Hall of Fame" for just about everything imaginable? We crave some form of recognition or purpose to validate our lives. We grasp for some measure of meaning, some aspect of immortality, to say we were here. I believe this yearning in our hearts is the longing for lost glory. It is a glory we possessed in the Garden of Eden that was lost in mankind's separation from God. We were created for so much more than what exists in this fallen world, but our search for satisfaction forever eludes us. I'm reminded of the words spoken by General George Patton: "All glory is fleeting."

Yet I have seen a glory that does not fade. I have seen a glory that does not leave you wanting for more. I have seen a glory that is greater than anything one can imagine. I have been in the presence of this unspeakable glory and I know for certain that this glory is available to each one of us just for the asking. You can know for yourself what I am saying is true.

SPECIAL THANKS TO . . .

The Holy Spirit
My wife and editor, Deborah
Terry Constant, God's man and my friend
Alli who captured the spirit in her art
and
Would someone please tell Malcolm Smith
that I was one of his researchers?

PREFACE

The Mystery

    A few years back, I determined I would never write another book. Though I enjoy writing, it's been all work with little reward. I have spent thousands of hours analyzing and documenting the events in my life in order to grasp "the Truth," all with the idea in mind that "the Truth would set me free." If I could grasp it and package it, I would be able to point me, and others, in the right direction. I figured if I worked hard and long enough I would receive the keys to the kingdom—I would possess "the Truth." Then, just as I would find the pieces of the puzzle coming together—the Truth at my fingertips—life's circumstances would send my puzzle crashing to the floor, thus shattering my picture in dozens of directions.

    The philosophy of working hard and long has achieved results in my business, a sales organization in which I have established hundreds of clients. Most of my clients buy from me because they think I know what I'm talking about. Maybe I do or maybe I don't, I'm really not sure, but one thing I know for certain—when it comes to my personal and intimate relationship with the Lord God Almighty, I really don't have a clue where He is going to lead me tomorrow. I only know from where I came and where I stand today. Grasping and packaging God just doesn't work.

    Looking back over my life, I stand in utter awe and amazement. If ever there was a man who was transformed from a life of death and bondage to a life of freedom and joy, it is I. Without a doubt, I have looked up more dead hogs' asses (Please pardon the expression, but it is an apt analogy!) than anyone you will ever meet. I have pursued more dead ends (and with zeal, I might add) only to come up empty. Yet my life as I know it now is full of grace and purpose, and I possess a true sense of well-being.

That's the good news. The bad news is I'm not sure how I got here other than God's mysterious and wonderful grace.

It simply boggles my mind how life is so full of twists and turns. When I finally gave up trying to put the pieces together, I found *the* piece—that piece being a truly intimate relationship with the living God. If there's one thing I have learned, it's that although you can't package or grasp God, you can know Him intimately. Anyone who truly knows God knows He is a God of love. Not only does God love us, He absolutely wants the very best for us. If you currently do not know that God loves you, I have good news for you! If you are sincere in your desire to really know who God is, you can come to know the love of God. I can also tell you with certainty that God will never impose His will on you in any way that is a violation to you. He won't force you to do anything. Love never violates another person. With God, you will have to choose, and that choice is essentially a choice for life.

I cannot tell you specifically what your relationship with God will look like, as this is between you and God. You cannot attain an intimate relationship with God if you rely on someone else to do it for you. We can never do it for someone else. When it comes to my personal relationship with the living God, I stand alone before God and so do you. We think we should be afraid of our nakedness, when in reality we are all naked before God. Standing alone and naked makes us nervous, however, so we construct idols in our lives to keep us from facing this truth. We fight over our belief systems while gripping our Bibles tenaciously, as though we are gaining some special favor with God. We think, "If I can *prove* myself right, I *must* be 'right' with God." Jesus addressed the futility of such behavior when He spoke these very harsh words about our self-important activities: "So you also outwardly appear righteous to men, but within you are full of hypocrisy and iniquity."[1]

Although I cannot define your relationship, I can tell you with certainty what will *not* work in this quest for an intimate relationship with God. Religion, for example, will not work. Religion did not work for the Pharisees when Jesus came on the scene, and things haven't changed one bit since then. Mixing up our roles won't work either. I have to be me, and God *will* be God. I don't know why this has been so hard for me to get, but it has.

Well, maybe I have an idea. I like being in control, and I'm not talking about self-control, one of the fruits of the spirit. I'm talking about being in control of my world, which of course isn't my world at all. Having to trust God when everything around me is crumbling or not going my way is not my idea of happiness. Looking back over my history, I have spent far more time trying to help God do His job than I have working on me and doing mine. Mixing up our roles simply won't work.

Denial also will not promote an intimate relationship with God—claiming all is right with the Lord or with our lives, when in fact one is living on the edge of despair. It's like being in a bad marriage and pretending everything's fine. There are activities, niceties, and idle conversation, but there's no passion, growth, or intimacy, and inside we feel the pain of loneliness and hopelessness. Filling our lives with church activities and quoting "positive" verses from the Bible to mask our pain and spiritual disconnection may fool others (and even ourselves for awhile), but God always knows the true nature of our hearts and the pain that we bear.

This book is about retracing my steps and looking at the miraculous ways in which God has healed me and given me new life. This book is also about hope. I'm going to share with you events in my life that may be hard for you to believe. They are hard for me to believe, and they happened to me! The real miracle of my life, however, does not lie in the arena of the sensational, but rather in the overwhelming sense of well-being that I now possess. For a good portion of my life I did not know that God loved me; as a matter of fact, I fought with God for more years than I care to remember. I felt I was on a bicycle peddling into a 50 mile-an-hour head wind. Now I feel like I'm on that same bike, but I have the wind at my back. I now know that I am utterly and completely loved and accepted by God.

I encourage you to come along on the ride with me. Be prepared to be challenged by what you read from time to time. Facing our true nature head-on is never easy. This book is for those people who are struggling and want to be set free. Free to be the person the Lord created you to be. Facing who you are with all your flaws and imperfections and knowing that God absolutely loves and accepts you is complete freedom. Before I take you on this journey, I want you to know my prayer for you is this:

> "Lord Jesus, I am so thankful for the miraculous healing You have performed in my life. Give me the words, Lord, to share that healing grace with all my brothers and sisters who are in need of a word from You. I know apart from the Holy Spirit, nothing is made straight. True love and joy come from You alone. I ask You, Father, to touch each person who longs for an intimate connection with You. And may the mystery of Your healing power be manifest in their lives as it has been in mine."

Chapter 1: The Holy Spirit

We have to get something straight right from the beginning: ***It is impossible to intimately know the love of God apart from the Person of the Holy Spirit.*** Notice I said "Person"; not doctrine, creed, or belief system. Before Jesus went to the cross, He prepared His disciples for His departure with these words: "I tell you the truth: it is to your advantage that I go away. For if I do not go, the counselor will not come to you."[2] Of course, Jesus was talking about the presence of the Holy Spirit, which He had clarified earlier, saying: "The Holy Spirit will teach you all things."[3]

Notice Jesus did not say, "Don't worry guys—after I leave, I'm going to leave you several copies of the Torah so you can get together and study the Old Testament, and then you'll know what to do." Nor did He say, "You're going to be lost for a time until Paul comes on the scene and writes a good portion of the New Testament. Then you can get together and study his work so you'll know what to do." No, Jesus was very emphatic: it's better that I go so the Father will send to you the Holy Spirit.

Yet who is the Holy Spirit? I don't mean intellectually who is the Holy Spirit—I am talking about truly understanding the purpose and nature and Person of the Holy Spirit. When an individual accepts Jesus Christ as the Lord and Savior of his life, he is promised that he will receive the Holy Spirit. Jesus came to deliver us from the bondage of sin and death, which was accomplished by His death and resurrection. Mel Gibson's movie *The Passion of the Christ* illustrates Jesus' purpose in coming as well as anything I have ever seen. In essence, Jesus came to create a new race of people, reconnected to the love of God, with the seal of that relationship being the Holy Spirit. We are taught and comforted by the Holy Spirit, and our intimate connection with

God is manifested through His Spirit. The Holy Spirit is our personal counselor who guides us in this new life.

In one true sense, trying to explain the Holy Spirit is like trying to explain the mystery of God, but I can illustrate how He has worked in my life. I am madly and passionately in love with my wife, and she is truly the love of my life. We are intimate soul mates, and she is God's choice for me, but still there is a problem. On occasion, an issue will present itself and we just don't agree. Neither one of us is good at submitting to people in general. As for myself, I won't submit to any person unless I understand what's going on. Neither will she. My wife has her own company, employing over 90 people—she likes being the boss. I also have my own company—and I like being the boss. She likes things her way, and I like things my way. Most importantly, each of us thinks we're right when it comes to a disagreement.

The sad truth of the matter is this: we wouldn't make it together for a week if we weren't submitted to Jesus Christ. I'm not talking about the *idea* of being submitted—I'm talking about *fully* submitting our wills to Jesus—desiring His will more than our own.

When we really lock horns to a point where neither one of us will give an inch, we know we're in trouble. All kinds of emotions usually come to the surface. My anger and withdrawal and her fragile sensitivity will flood us, so we find ourselves turning to the Lord. We find a quiet place, get down on our knees, and pray. It's not that we want to pray, because we don't. Actually, it's the last thing in the world I want to do, but we both know if God doesn't show up, the peace in our marriage will be destroyed and our marriage ultimately will not survive. Every time we have done this, and I mean *every* time (without *any* exceptions), God has shown up and answered us. Usually it's immediate, sometimes after an hour or two, and on rare occasions it may take an evening, but He always shows up.

Sometimes I discover I'm the bad guy. Sometimes she's the bad guy. Both of us absolutely hate being the bad guy, because the bad guy is "wrong" and we like being right. Personally, I would rather eat dirt than be the bad guy in an argument with my wife. It's so easy to be sweet and forgiving when the other person is wrong, but when you find yourself at fault, acknowledging the problem is not so effortless. However, when I am the bad guy and the Holy Spirit points out my problem, all I can really say is I'm sorry because I just couldn't see my mistake without His help. Sometimes it's a bit disorienting—thinking you are right when, in fact, you are wrong. It's like the Holy Spirit shines a light into a darkened room of my life.

    I am always amazed when I see a spiritual transformation take place within myself. Basically the process looks like this: first of all, I'm absolutely convinced I'm right, and I can defend my position like a trial attorney. Sometimes I quote verses from the Bible to prove my point. The next step is the frustrating realization that I am getting nowhere with my argument. As a matter of fact, things are getting worse! Enter in the feelings of anger, isolation and separation—all feelings of death. It is the pain of this downward spiral that causes me to turn to the Lord. Getting on my knees is an act of submission, and in this state I truly submit my will to the Lord. He comes in and shows me the error of my thinking, which usually reflects a self-righteous attitude that has nothing to do with love. At this point, my perspective completely changes. Several hours after this takes place, my original position, which caused the problem in the first place, now looks completely absurd. The best way I can describe the transformation is that the spirit which was disconnected from God's love is put to death and is replaced by a spirit of love and life. Simply amazing! God is actually creating something new in me, and that newness is connected to His Spirit.

    Keep in mind, you don't need much information in order to communicate with the living God. The Holy Spirit will be your best friend once you get to know Him. There are, however, two things that are essential if you truly want to be intimate with God. First, you have to be honest, and by that I mean you have to be yourself, just as God made you. Second, you have to be willing to accept God's very best for you. In reality, He is your Father and absolutely loves you.

Chapter 2: The Spirit of Death

Just as you cannot know the love of God apart from the Holy Spirit, it is imperative to know there are spirits in this world that are not united with God. Like it or not, we are involved in spiritual warfare. Satan and demonic forces do exist. Often Satan will appear to us as an angel of light, and it is easy to be deceived by his power. The love of God is undeniable, however, and it is essential that His presence be distinguished from unholy beings.

I'm going to share an experience from my life that underscores the importance of this point. The narrative of events reads more like a novel because it's written from the perspective of how I saw the events unfolding at the time—how they actually appeared to me. There will undoubtedly be those who will not believe my story, although every word is true. Before the Lord, I swear everything I have written is accurate, with no embellishment. At this time in my life, I did not believe in a place called Hell. I was a Christian—I knew Jesus was Lord and I believed in the resurrection—but I was so disillusioned with religion that I had thrown out the entire package of Christian dogma and doctrine. The implications of what took place have had a profound impact on my life. I hope this story will touch your life as well.

The Year 1987

I had been retained by members of a Dallas firm to negotiate a business settlement with a former partner (whom I had never met), who lived in Kauai, Hawaii. For purposes of this narrative, I'll call this man "Alf." The Dallas firm wanted Alf out of their organization. The legal papers had been drawn up and the settlement seemed equitable, even generous, from my perspective. When they spoke of Alf, they were apprehensive, exhibiting uneasiness about the negotiations. They were skittish and evasive, emanating a sense of fear. But it was more than that—something I couldn't put my finger on; I just sensed it. One of the partners who hired me later confessed that he had felt I would not come back alive.

As the events of my trip began to unfold, I came to understand the reason for the fear and uneasiness. After boarding the DC-10 at the Los Angeles airport for my flight to Hawaii, I reviewed the events of the day. I had encountered trouble with my connecting flight from Houston, which delayed me getting into Los Angeles and caused me to miss my original flight to Honolulu. Then, there was that unsettling moment in the Los Angeles terminal when Alf, who was supposed to pick me up at the airport in Kauai, was paged over the airport paging system. *"Strange,"* I thought. I was relieved to be on a nearly empty plane, but as the engines roared and we headed down the runway, I felt an uneasiness I could not explain. I tried to dismiss it. *"Nonsense,"* I thought and rested my head against the seat. I had been a Sergeant in the Marine Corps and spent 14 months in Vietnam. I worked my way through college as a police officer. I was also highly trained in the art of self-defense and skilled in various forms of weaponry. I did not believe in intimidating anyone, and others did not intimidate me. I would soon discover how completely wrong I was.

After landing in Honolulu, I caught a shuttle jumper to Kauai. When I landed on the small island, it was dark and raining. It had been arranged for me to stay with the mysterious Alf, and I wondered what he looked like. I sensed his power from the attitude of those who hired me and knew from what they said that he was wealthy. Would he arrive in a limousine? Was his home perched on some hillside overlooking the beautiful blue Pacific? I played with the speculations, and then drove them away. I had a job to do, and his being a powerful man meant little to me.

I placed a call to Alf's residence. He was on his way. I stacked my luggage neatly under the protection of the rain-soaked canopy and waited for his arrival. Calmly placing a cigarette in my mouth, I watched the raindrops as they splattered against the pavement.

Suddenly, as if out of nowhere, Alf appeared in front of me. We shook hands, and Alf introduced himself. He was small in stature with a pleasant, attractive face. His manner was unobtrusive. I smiled to myself as we walked across the parking lot. What could my employers possibly have feared? Alf seemed nice enough and certainly harmless. It didn't make sense. We chatted and exchanged the usual niceties. When we reached his vehicle, I stopped dead in my tracks. The limo I had half expected turned out to be a gutted VW van that was totally stripped down. "*Strange*," I thought and climbed in.

On the way to Alf's place, I asked if he drank. It had been a long day for me, and a drink sounded good. When he informed me he did not, I asked him to stop at a liquor store. I purchased a fifth of bourbon, and once again we were on our way. The narrow streets flew by quickly under the tires of his speeding van. He was forging his way into the winding hills, and I was consciously recording the directions. But soon, the odd twists and turns he made on the back roads became impossible to track. It became obvious that Alf was taking some course that would be impossible to recall. Tall sugar cane lined the road, blocking my view. The van finally stopped and before me, in a small clearing surrounded by sugar cane, stood a shack. I briefly pondered the situation and then unloaded my bags.

The shack looked vacant from the outside and appeared to be under construction. The interior had concrete floors with sawdust scattered about. A central room contained a hot plate, a sink, a few chairs, and a makeshift shower.

Alf immediately started to talk business. "Please, not tonight," I said apologetically. "It's been a long day." "*And now this mess*," I thought.

We chatted briefly. I drank some healthy shots of bourbon and went to bed on a cot that was hidden behind a curtain.

In the morning, I awoke fresh and alert. I went outside to smoke a cigarette and get a sense of where I was on the island. The shack was completely surrounded by sugar cane fields. Junk was strewn around the small yard. A chicken coop stood close by. In the distance was a mountain scattered with homes. There was a distinctive yellow house on the side of the mountain. I took my bearings and planted them deeply in my mind. I could get out if necessary and I could get back. It might take a helicopter, but I could return to the shack if things turned bad.

  We ate a tasteless breakfast that Alf prepared. "What's with the rooster in the paper bag?" I inquired, pointing to a wounded rooster that was confined in a bag. "Sick," was the extent of his reply. Although I didn't realize it at the time, I now believe that the wounded rooster was to be used as a sacrifice in some occult ritual. During a subsequent vacation in Kauai over the Christmas holidays, my friends and I found it was impossible to order chicken at the local restaurants. I was informed by one of the locals (who, I might add, was very reluctant to speak) that Christmas was a time for sacrifice to the demons of darkness. You won't find *that* information in any tour guide. But, I digress; so let's get back to my story.

  We started to talk about the state of affairs in the world. The discussion went on for hours on end. There was a kind of disturbing arrogance and brilliance in much of his thinking. Many things he voiced sounded "true" on the surface, steeped in correctness and self-righteousness, but left me with a growing sense of frustration and discomfort. He had formulated answers to many of the world's problems. A world monetary system was one of his pet theories. He thought meaningless paperwork and consumerism were at the heart of America's problems, along with a lack of morality. People were liars and thieves. "There's no productivity," he declared. The answer, he thought, called for sacrifice. On and on we talked, but his ideology seemed to run in large, complex circles and always looped back to himself. People were mere objects to Alf—human machines to implement his grandiose plans. "People are like ants," he theorized. "We all live in one big ant mound. Of course there are drones, workers who scurry about, and every mound has its queen."

  Intermittently he would rage about the business partners who had sent me. "Thieves, liars, all of them…" he would rant.

They had taken what was his. He had trusted them, and they had betrayed him. How I wondered? I tried a different tactic. I asked him if he wanted it all back, and he looked stunned.

"What do you mean?" he asked.

"Do you want it all back?" I inquired rhetorically, and then continued. "Yes, there are hundreds of thousands of dollars in inventory, but you are ignoring the fact that there are also hundreds of thousands of dollars in liabilities." I was bluffing and simply looking for some way to move forward with the negotiations.

"I don't want to be involved in running any of the business," he said. "I just want my rightful share." The problem with this was there was no "rightful share" that didn't include a tremendous amount of work, restructuring and liability and Alf wanted none of these. Alf wanted easy cash.

"*Like the queen in the ant hill*," I thought, but said nothing.

It was growing dark, and we had been talking since breakfast, with no attempt on his part to extend human graciousness. He finally asked what I would like for dinner, yet the tone of his question was cold and hollow. I could feel my resentment growing. Everything appeared to be something it wasn't. I told him it wasn't important what we ate, and I meant it. We had sparred with countless words and ideas, but I was really never a part of the conversation. He was like a robot that could answer his own questions. The questions and answers ran in circles—always back to him. Eating together would not be any different. I would be eating alone even if we shared the same table.

I was tiring of the empty games, even though a battle of words can be of great interest to me. My interest turned into contempt. He was void of any real substance, and he exhibited no compassion. "What sustains you?" I finally asked him, point-blank.

"What do you mean?" he replied with surprise.

"I have always been fascinated by human motivation," I said. "Why people do what they do. When I look at you, listen to you, I wonder what keeps you from blowing your brains out." I meant every word of this.

He smiled at me, a sly and knowing look. The words slid smoothly from his mouth. "I have a symbiotic relationship with the higher spiritual powers, and they are not good; they are not human." His eyes narrowed, "They serve me, and I serve them. We have a relationship based on mutual respect."

When he spoke there was an extraordinary force of energy in the room that I couldn't understand nor define. But I knew what he was saying was true, as crazy as it seemed. *(I later learned some interesting background information on Alf. Alf's father, an SS officer in Germany during World War II, had been deeply involved in the occult. His mother, a Catholic, was part of the Dutch resistance. When Alf was six years old, he followed in his father's footsteps and renounced Christianity.)*

"Our business is terminated," I immediately informed him.
"What?"
"I'm out of here right now."
"You have failed in the negotiations," Alf sneered mockingly.
"Yes I have. And I will take full responsibility for that failure. Take me to the airport now, or I am walking my way out of here."

As he drove me toward the airport he interrupted the silence. "Don't be too hasty in your decision," he remarked in a quiet tone of voice. "Sleep on it tonight and consider giving me a call in the morning." Alf dropped me off at the airport, quickly reiterating, "Sleep on it," and sped away. I felt better just from the release of his presence, but my mental wheels were spinning.

I couldn't begin to grasp the overwhelming mental and emotional grind I'd been through. I was physically and emotionally worn out. There had been something so inhuman in all of it. There was an unreality in my consciousness about what I had experienced—like a nightmare from which you can't awake. It was terrifying in a way that words can't adequately describe. With further thought, it seemed real and unreal at the same time. I had no mental category to shed light on what I had experienced.

As I recall this incident, I do not know exactly why I chose to stay, but I decided to spend the night in Kauai and start fresh in the morning. Perhaps I was just exhausted. Perhaps, in part, I was ashamed of failing in the negotiations. There was nothing to report that didn't sound like voodoo. No one would believe me. Also, I was not the kind of man to run from anything. Unbeknownst to me at the time, I would ultimately flee in the face of terror that I had never known before.

    I rented a car at the airport and asked the agent to recommend the best hotel in the area. She was very helpful and provided maps and directions to the nearby Hilton Hotel, which was located on the water. I wanted to hug her, but, of course, I didn't. She was just so human, so normal, so real.

    Arriving at the hotel, I cheerfully asked the lady at the front desk for the best room they had. Surprisingly, money didn't matter to me that night. I say surprisingly, as I am usually very frugal with money. This is particularly true when it comes to other people's money, even when I am given an open-ended expense account. I ate an expensive, delicious dinner and then walked down to the beach to clear my mind. The night sky was clear and the stars and moon were shining brightly. I walked along the surf and lost track of time.

    Back in my room, the sickening sense of paranoia returned. I wanted to talk to someone, but I didn't know what to say. I am usually willing to talk about anything, but I sounded nuts, even to myself. I decided to call my wife (my second wife), but the moment I heard her voice I knew something was wrong.

    She said she didn't know what was happening to her. I tried to calm her. There was panic in her voice. She relayed the events of the previous night. She had been so scared, totally paralyzed by fear. She had locked herself in the bedroom and had huddled by the side of the bed with my revolver, a .357 Magnum. When I asked her what she was afraid of she couldn't explain it. Like me, she'd been caught in a strange and frightening void. She said she'd been worried sick about me, but didn't know why.

    I relayed only part of my story, not wanting to cause her more anxiety, and then spoke some reassuring words. I hung up and agonized over the conversation and events of my trip, trying to pull the pieces of the puzzle together.

The next morning, feeling disoriented and leery, I phoned Alf and he agreed to meet at the restaurant in the airport terminal to discuss further the negotiations. He inquired about my flight arrangements, but I avoided the question, not wanting to share any more information than was absolutely necessary with this man that I had come to loathe. He continued to show an unusual preoccupation with my flight plans, asking more than once during the phone conversation. I finally told him with sincerity that I would be flying on "Haloalu Airlines," naming a fictitious airline. He repeated "Haloalu" casually without hesitation or comment.

I packed my bags and checked out of the room. After returning the rental car, I checked my luggage, confirmed my flight, and proceeded to the restaurant where Alf and I had agreed to meet. It was a gorgeous day, without a cloud in the sky, but the beautiful weather did not buoy my dark mood. Not since my days in Vietnam or my hair-raising experiences as a police officer had I felt such a sense of uneasiness—every nerve and muscle in my body was on alert. It was like going to war with an unseen enemy.

Alf was late and I smoked one cigarette after another, trying to summon a sense of calmness and control that continued to elude me. I had picked a corner table, with my back to the wall, so I could clearly see both entrances to the restaurant.

When Alf finally appeared, he asked pleasantly enough, "Where did you stay last night?"

"The Hilton," I responded without enthusiasm. I was in no mood for small talk.

He smiled an accusing smile. "Consumerism. Do you like to spend money?" he taunted.

"I enjoy nice things." I answered flatly. He started to take off on this topic but I interrupted and said, "Let's get down to business."

He smiled. "O.K. You show me yours, and I'll show you mine."

I pulled the legal documents from the small attaché case I was carrying. Briefly, I ran down all the details of the settlement.

"This was all planned before you arrived," he said in a caustic manner.

"Of course," I replied. "Yesterday I said you could have all of the business; but, you didn't want any of it. The individuals I represent only want one-fourth, and they don't want to do business with you any more."

He then showed me his proposal. It was completely unworkable and he knew it.

He knew I wouldn't buy any of it. Upon receiving my negative answer, he abruptly stood and left without another word. I felt numb and a sense of unreality washed over me. Then I noticed, or rather became aware of, a man standing some distance from me. Although he was not looking directly at me, I knew that he was completely focused on me. He continued to move closer to me, his outward manner casual, but a dark power emanated from him that filled me with an unexplainable dread.

Terror hit me with full force. The very marrow of my bones seemed to melt. Fear clawed at me. I stumbled from the table and moved into the corridor outside the restaurant. Two security guards stood by their station, but as I moved toward them, I didn't know what to say. There was an insane, irrational and paralyzing edge to my terror.

I fled down the corridor, jumped the guardrails, and slowed my pace. My fear began to abate enough for me to think rationally again. I instinctively knew that Alf and this man watching me were aware of my flight plans. I had to get on a different plane than the one on which I was scheduled, but I wanted to avoid the ticket counters. I caught sight of Alf moving quickly down the hall, looking for me. I pressed my back against a pillar and went in the opposite direction. I felt as though I was caught in the middle of some unreal horror movie. I didn't believe in evil spirits, but the only way to describe the spirit coming out of Alf and this other man was evil.

At the end of the long hallway, one of the planes was boarding for the main island. It was *not* my flight. "Please stand back," an attendant was pleading. "We have overbooked this flight. We need volunteers to take the next flight." I eased to the side of the crowd of people, slipped behind the attendant, and walked onto the plane. I spied an empty seat and quickly grabbed it. A harried flight attendant was insistent. "Some of you will have to reschedule," she said, waving tickets. "There are not enough seats……" I said nothing and didn't move. People were quarreling, demanding their places. When the plane took off, I was miraculously still on it.

Chapter 3: A Miraculous Glimpse behind the Curtain

As miraculous as it was for me to be on that plane, God was about to perform a miracle that was incomparable in magnitude and clarity to anything I had previously experienced, other than, perhaps, the miracle of my original conversion. At some point during my trip from Kauai to the main island of Hawaii there was a break—a moment, or moments—when time stood still. I cannot define this experience in terms of time; I can only say that in those moments, I was ushered into another dimension. God momentarily drew back the curtain that separates our physical world from the spiritual world. What I saw and experienced in this spiritual world was crystal clear: I was shown *light* and *darkness* and I began to understand, with amazement, the absolute reality of good and evil, of Heaven and Hell.

Of Darkness

In a moment of suspended time I saw a place of *darkness*—a black hole of inexhaustible depth. Cavernous, endless expressions of appetite existed with nothing to dull the monstrous desires. Unlike our human existence where Satan is able to empower those who have submitted to him to feed off of the pain and suffering of others—such as the Nazi war movement or the psychopathic mind that feels sexual excitement when mutilating its victim—there was nothing to feed or empower the vast dark desires of the souls that existed in this place. Nothing of God or goodness was found there. Love, compassion, and hope did not exist. It was absolutely empty of joy, with a sense of unspeakable horror. Yet there was a consciousness of death, oozing pain with nothing to diminish the terror. There was no escape of any kind.

Although the experience was surreal, one thing I know for certain: **To be separated from the love of God is absolute and unspeakable death.** This revelation of Hell posed no personal threat to me, as I was fully aware that I belong to God, but the revulsion and disgust I felt at this pervasive *darkness* seemed more than my soul could bear. For months later, I earnestly prayed that God would erase the memories from my mind forever.

Of Light

On the heels of *darkness*, I was suddenly surrounded with inexpressible *Light* and Love. Words cannot begin to express the Glory that surrounded me. The magnitude and intensity of the Glory of this Love was unfathomable. It was not so much what I saw—as human eyes have no comparable experience—but what I felt. I experienced an infusion of unimaginable joy and jubilation. It was a vision of radiant beauty, a magnificent splendor, surpassing all dimension or comprehension. Peace was triumphal and celebration all encompassing. All I can do is babble around what I saw and felt.

This was a place of Everlasting Life—Life beyond our human understanding; Life beyond our wildest hopes or dreams of what Heaven may be. People here were made gloriously whole. There was no judgment, no sin, and no religious morality. A pure and constant Love existed in perfect harmony in a place of perfect splendor. Those suspended moments, bathed in the Light of Heaven, left me with an abiding sense of hope and joy about the home that God has prepared for us.

Chapter 4: The Aftermath

As the engines slowed for our descent to Honolulu, I was totally focused on getting home as quickly as possible. After landing, I headed for the main terminal and reviewed the departure schedule. I was delighted to see there was a flight to Dallas-Fort Worth in less than two hours. I waited in line, excited with the thought of getting out of there. The lady behind the counter gave me a friendly smile, checked the computer, and confirmed that she could get me on the flight. I exhaled with relief and handed her my credit card. After a few moments she informed me that she could not accept my card, which made no sense, as I knew I had plenty of credit remaining. I handed her another credit card. This credit card also mysteriously failed to pass clearance, yet it was also far below its limit. The same happened with all my credit cards—the agent said she was unable to accept any of them.

Flustered, and somewhat embarrassed, I started to pay by check, but the ticket agent declined to accept this method of payment, also. I then asked to see her supervisor, but the supervisor also refused to help. Neither woman would offer any rational explanation for the denial—just the statement that they couldn't accept my credit cards or my check. I couldn't believe what I was hearing. It made absolutely no sense. Satan was still in pursuit, but the love of Jesus continued to sustain me. I remained calm and searched my mind for a solution.

"Give me an hour," I told the agent. "Keep my name on the reservation list." I hurried to a phone booth and called my wife. "Are you all right?" she asked, with a desperate tone in her voice. "I don't have time to explain anything," I said. "I need you to go to DFW and prepay a ticket for me. Now." My wife did as I asked and purchased my ticket with a check. The ticket agent in Dallas also checked and verified that there was no problem with the limit on our credit cards. The woman could give no explanation for my disheartening and irritating experience with the same airline in

Honolulu. Just a few minutes before the final boarding call, I was given clearance to board the plane that would take me home.

The plane took off and I leaned back in my seat and relaxed for the first time since I'd left home. If the captain had informed us that he needed to ditch the plane into the sea, I would have felt no fear. Terror such as I had never known before was behind me. Satan and the demonic forces that had come against me were defeated. The Spirit of God's love returned to me and I could feel it infuse every cell of my being, erasing all sense of shame or doubt. I felt truly free for the first time in my life. I sensed people's needs. I wanted to get out of my seat and go up to people on that plane and ask them specific questions and let them know they are loved by their Creator. "Are you a drug addict?" I would have asked one. "A homosexual?" to another. There were people on that flight who had pain and rejection etched into their faces. I wanted to throw my arms around them and tell them how much God truly loved them.

****

My final contact with Alf came shortly after I safely returned to Dallas. Within a week of my return, I received an unsolicited phone call from Alf. I had already determined that if Alf ever pursued me, one of us was going to die. I could have killed Alf if he threatened me or any member of my family and would have felt no more remorse than one would feel after killing a rabid rat. I informed him on the phone that I never wanted to speak to him again. At that point, he said something interesting to me: "You're just one of those purists who don't approve of my tactics. I guess you are one of God's elect." I have not heard from Alf since.

Frankly, his words are still confusing, but they hit at the heart of the issue. First of all, I am far more profane than I am pure, so my personal purity has nothing to do with being one of "God's elect." Second, the idea of being one of God's elect is a theological concept that no one I know really understands. Maybe

Alf did, or does, I don't know. But this I do know—the spirit empowering and controlling Alf was real and hideously evil. Personally, I believe Alf was amazed that I didn't submit to this evil authority. He himself was a weak shell of a man and possessed no power or authority in and of himself. Man to man, I could have kicked his ass all over the island. But this wasn't man to man. Maybe nothing really is, I don't know. I am convinced that in and of myself, this malevolent force would have crushed me.

Like it or not, we are all involved in spiritual warfare. If it had not been for the *Spirit of life, which dwells within me*, I would have been destroyed by the powerful force of evil that had devoured Alf. The same holds true for me today. It was the reality of Jesus that sustained me then and it is the reality of Jesus that sustains me now.

****

It has been 18 years since that fateful trip to Kauai. The events of that trip began a transformation in me that continues to this day, providing a path of profound healing and growth. Prior to making that trip, I had come to believe that Hell did not exist. I had thrown religious dogma, ideas and formulas out the door and I didn't believe much of anything, although I was still connected to Jesus. After that trip and God's miraculous enlightening of my mind, I *knew* Hell existed. My worst nightmares were a walk in the park compared to what I had seen. It was like viewing unimaginable and endless death.

The vision of Heaven, on the other hand, was unimaginable Glory and I cling to the memory with a sense of wonderment and awe. I still remember how I became overwhelmed by the Glory of God I witnessed. His Glory is unspeakable majesty and splendor that fills me with a sense of peace and joy and purpose.

Since that trip in 1987, I have never questioned the goodness and righteousness of God. The world we live in knows little to nothing of God's Glory. The best of this world looks like a burned out junkyard in comparison to the Heaven that awaits us.

Ironically, for most of my life, I held God responsible for countless perceived injustices. If God really is God, I previously reasoned, how could He allow all the pain and suffering in this world? I used to think about my own suffering. In my mind, God had a lot to answer for. I can't count the number of times I railed at God for everything bad in this world. Somehow, miraculously, as a result of the events of that trip, I have been silenced. It's not that everything makes sense to me now, because it doesn't. I don't suddenly have all the answers. I don't posses the "truth" in the way that I tried so desperately to possess at one time. But once you have been in the presence of God, you will never again question His loving kindness.

Chapter 5: The Holy Spirit's Purpose

We have a natural tendency to divide people between good guys and bad guys, sinners and saints. When a man tells me he has a symbiotic relationship with what he calls "higher powers—and they're not good," it doesn't take a rocket scientist to know he is intimate with evil. And if one is intimate with evil, one is intimate with Satan and demons. I know that such people will reap their "just reward."

But what about me? What about my tendencies and bents that can be harmful? When the Holy Spirit reveals a particular attitude of non-love in my life, I never see a pretty picture of myself. Though I no longer measure myself or others using a standard of goodness or badness, if I had to choose a label for myself, I would say I am bad. I know my wife would agree. The fact remains, I am a "sinner" and I often make mistakes.

I find there is more confusion in the Christian community over the topic of sin than any other issue, and the only way I know to deal with sin is to address it head-on. First of all, let me say that the Holy Spirit was not given to us to make us feel guilty.

Guilt is about condemnation, but in Christ, there is no condemnation[4]. Satan is called "the accuser of the brethren" and sometimes these relentless accusations can be debilitating. People who have not known genuine love or have been abused and those who have been trapped in legalism seem especially susceptible to these attacks of Satan. Know with absolute certainty that these attacks are not from the Lord, although Satan will present them as such. If you are plagued with guilt and can't seem to shake these feelings, get a loving friend to pray over you, as these accusations are not from God. My sin and your sin were taken care of at the cross, and when Jesus rose from the dead, it was over. Finished. End of conversation!

Many people do not truly understand the resurrected new life we have in Christ. Resurrection for Christians starts the day they accept Jesus Christ as Lord and Savior. We then have a lifetime of choices to make which bring about spiritual health or sickness, and one of the Holy Spirit's purposes is to help us understand those choices. Some of the most miserable people I know are born-again Christians who have either made destructive choices, ignoring the prompting of the Holy Spirit, or who truly do not understand what their choices are, often because they have not experienced a healthy concept of love. God's loving kindness through the work of the Holy Spirit is opening my eyes to the true meaning of being a Christian. The Christian life is all about choices.

Though the Holy Spirit will never make us feel guilty, the issue of Godly sorrow certainly exists. Godly sorrow, which leads to repentance, is totally connected to love, unlike guilt, which leaves you feeling condemned and without any choices. In another respect, guilt is also all about "me and my feelings," which may partially come about because of my unwillingness to accept God's grace in absolving my guilt. Focusing on me rather than on grace then creates a deeper hole, as "me," separated from God, is basically the problem. Godly sorrow, on the other hand, points us to repentance and is always a path to life, freedom and joy. Repentance means I am turning away from the harm I have caused. This includes harm I have done to myself, as God created us to love ourselves. Repentance is about changing and accepting the new spirit Jesus has for me. Repentance is about love.

The Holy Spirit for a Christian is really all about love, but God's love is much, much broader than our limited, romantic notions of love. God's love changes us from the inside out—which is the essence of the resurrected new life. For me, it looks something like this: I have ceased thinking of myself as being good or bad. I am simply me and God is God. God is truly my best friend and my Father. He knows me better than anyone, including myself, and He loves me. I am not afraid of Him. He won't give in to my occasional tantrums, but I throw them anyway. For the most part, what people think of me really doesn't matter because I am completely accepted by the One who does matter. I'm glad I'm me, and when I think about the God who loves me, I get those feelings of *Glory*—and I have seen the *Glory* which awaits us. Your relationship may look completely different because we are all unique before God.

Believe me when I say I understand how confusing this concept of good and bad, of sinner and saint, can get—especially after some of the sermons I have heard. Legalism, which is characteristic of religion, is all about guilt, and legalism was (and is) conceived in the pit of hell. Take the apostle Paul, for example, who wrote a good portion of the New Testament. Paul certainly thought in terms of good guys and bad guys. Before Paul met Jesus on the road to Damascus, he was a Pharisee. In fact, by his own admission, he was the chief of Pharisees. *Numero uno*! In today's language, Paul would claim to be the most religious and righteous man alive. The Pharisees were all about keeping laws, commandments, and rules. Not just the Ten Commandments, mind you, but hundreds of other laws as well. The Pharisees performed these tasks at great sacrifice to themselves, all out of what appeared to be their dedication and devotion to God.

When Jesus showed up on the scene, however, He threw down the gauntlet and took on the religious leaders of His time. Jesus was not kind in his appraisal of those people—not kind at all. Jesus was clear in His distinction between faithfully following God and the deceptive rhetoric and activities of organized and self-imposed religion. He left little room for argument that the self-righteous practices of the Pharisees were, in fact, not holy at all. Most Pharisees hated Jesus for the words He spoke, and in the end they crucified Him. Not just crucified, but beat, humiliated, and tortured Him.

In his zeal as a religious man of his day, Paul continued trying to destroy the sect of people who called themselves Christians. This destruction was especially true concerning the Jewish Christians. Paul rightly understood that this new group led by the Holy Spirit was destroying his religious traditions. He thought he was killing Christians in the name of God, a necessary precaution to protect the sanctity of his religion. Of course, when Paul met the resurrected Jesus on the road to Damascus, this meeting threw a monkey wrench into his thinking. Personally, I laugh every time I think about this event. Can you imagine it? Paul is struck down by a blinding light and he knows the Glory surrounding him is the Glory of God. He cries out, "Who are you Lord?" And the answer comes back to him, "I am Jesus."[5] "I am Jesus!" Think about it! Paul thought he was God's number one religious servant, obediently killing Christians in the name of God. Now he has come face to face with the Lord of the Universe and the Lord answers him by simply saying, "I am Jesus." Believe me friends; Paul was not having a good day.

Paul was certainly a committed man; a man on fire—first as a Pharisee, then as a Christian. It is interesting to note how Paul viewed himself over the course of his life. At the beginning of Paul's Christian ministry, he called himself the least of the apostles[6]. He viewed himself as falling from number one out of thousands of Pharisees to dead last as an apostle. In the middle of his life and ministry, he called himself the least of all Christians[7]. Historians put the number of Christians at that time around 5,000. Notice the way Paul's view of himself was dropping fast. At the end of his life, Paul called himself the chief of sinners[8]. That means Paul saw himself as the worst person who had ever lived—number one bad guy. Don't you find this interesting? Over the course of Paul's life, he went from seeing himself as being one of the most righteous men on earth as a chief religious leader of his time to the worst person who ever lived. **So it is with every person who compares himself or herself to others in the light of the grace of God.** Ironically, many people today portray Paul as one of the greatest Christians of all time because he was responsible for writing much of the New Testament. Paul, however, viewed himself as the least of all Christians. As Christians, we often see ourselves as good guys or bad guys, but God sees us through eyes of perfect love and wants us to become who He created us to be.

There is no doubt that one of the purposes of the Holy Spirit is to help us grow—and that growth is all about love. God loves us as a father loves his child. Love is always about relationship. Growing up in our relationship with God is about growing in love. There are Christians today who are afraid of God because they feel they are not good enough. No matter how hard they try, they don't measure up to God's standards. If you are one of these people, you simply do not know who you are in Christ. You really do not understand God's perfect love for you and the new life you have in Christ.

    I am a dad, and some of the best relationships I have are with my grown children. However, I have a daughter with whom I have not spoken in over a year. There are problems in our relationship, but I completely love her and I like her. I couldn't love her any more than I already do, regardless of the state of our relationship or the choices she makes in life. Currently, she doesn't want to relate to me, and that's OK, although I miss her. If there is one thing of which I am absolutely positive, it is this: even though I love my daughter fully, God's love infinitely transcends my capacity for love. His love reigns on an unfathomable scale.

    We have all heard the story of Adam and Eve and of our exile from the Garden. For many, it's just a story and we take it lightly. In reality, however, it is not light at all. All fear and death originate from this event, and it's not just about apples. Let me briefly recap what took place.

    In the Garden of Eden, Satan promised that if we ate from the Tree of Knowledge we would be just like God, knowing good and evil. God knew that being independent from Him was death. God said that we would die and warned us not to eat from the Tree. When Adam and Eve chose to disobey God and ate of the forbidden fruit, mankind made the choice for independence. "You will be like God knowing good and evil."[9] After eating the fruit, their eyes were opened and they knew they were naked, so they hid in the garden. When God called out to them and asked why they were hiding, Adam responded with, "I was afraid."[10] Fear had been born in man! In its essence, fear is simply the result of being separated from God who is love.

    This is where all the good guy and bad guy stuff comes from. We have bought into the lie. Satan promises that we will be like God, knowing good and evil. And many people, millions actually, still believe the lie today. "I'm not good enough." "I'm not living up to the standards God has for me in the Bible." "Poor pitiful me." On the other hand, there are those who point out all they do for God to stay in His good favor. All of it is death, just as God promised.

    I tell you my friends, if we want to be free, we are going to have to get naked before God, clothed only in the love of Jesus. The Holy Spirit will guide you and you will learn how to intimately relate with your Father. For example, I personally never talk to God about guilt because I know guilt is a tool of Satan. Satan wants you and me to feel condemned. I may say a word or two to the demonic forces who try to torment me from time to time. I tell them where they can stick it and I remind them that their time is short—God has already prevailed. Believe me when I tell you demons know Jesus was resurrected and that this spiritual war is already over. Anyway, I don't talk to my Father about guilt because He doesn't make me feel guilty. I do talk to Him about my sex life, business, fishing, relationships, and everything else that is pertinent to my life. Sometimes I just chitchat and ramble.

    As for your intimate conversations with God, I don't have a clue what the two of you will discuss. Maybe you will have to talk about your feelings of guilt. I have no idea whatsoever where the Holy Spirit is going to lead you because you are different from me. We are each unique in the eyes of God. For example, although my wife and I are truly one in many ways, in many respects we are completely opposite personalities. Almost from the day I first met her to the present, I have known that we possess the same spirit when it comes to the Lord, yet she relates to God completely differently from the way I do. My wife rarely approaches God casually, as one would approach a friend. God, to her, is a Holy and loving Father and she tends to be reverent in her conversations with Him. Chitchat is not her style (at least not with the Lord, though she can chitchat with the best of them when it comes to her earthly relationships). She also tends to think more in terms of performance and her petitions include seeking God's guidance in showing her how to be a "good wife," a "good mother," a "good boss," a "good friend," a "good daughter," and a host of other "goods." She also frequently prays for wisdom and discernment. My wife has almost always understood her choices in life, as she was raised with real love. She says God does talk to her about obedience—not in a guilt-producing, heavy handed sort of way—but in the way a loving parent explains to a child why obedience is important. There was a time when she would pray with many words (she is good with words), asking for help and answers, giving thanks for various things, but not understanding that, even with God—most importantly with God, in fact—conversation is a two-way street. God cured her of this in a dramatic and poignant way.

Years ago she had been praying incessantly about gaining discernment regarding a particular issue that was bothering her. When God finally gave her clarity, she thanked Him and asked Him why it had taken so long to answer her prayer. She swears God answered, clearly, nearly audibly, "Because I couldn't get a word in edgewise!" She says she knows He was smiling when He said it and that she laughed in response. And then God laughed! Now, that's intimacy! My wife has learned to sit with the Lord at times without a prayer list or agenda. "Be still and know that I am God,"[11] has taken on a special meaning for her.

Although your conversations with the Lord will be unique, I know you will find this to be true of your relationship with Him: there are things which you can freely do before God that I can't (or shouldn't), and there are things which I can freely do before God that you can't (or shouldn't). The Bible addresses the reality of this principle in 1Corinthians 8:7-9. As a couple, my wife and I have had to work this out. We are truly intimate and talk about nearly everything, but we have learned to respect each other's boundaries. There are things we don't share with each other out of obedience to the Lord. Rather than producing bondage, this has always promoted freedom and life.

There is also the issue of God's timing in our lives—God is like a loving parent who patiently encourages us to grow and turn away from harmful behaviors. He doesn't punish or belittle us for being "infants" or for being slow learners. He does, however, expect us to grow, just as a parent expects his or her child to grow beyond certain childish behaviors. As we grow in our relationship and love with God, He reveals more of His will to us and asks for new levels of obedience—things that were acceptable in the past will no longer be acceptable in light of our continuing transformation. The process of transformation, which brings about healing and a resurrected, abundant life, is full of ups and downs. A good friend of mine says we grow and then there are plateaus. More often than not, our growth is born out of suffering. In the New Testament, Peter said this about suffering, "Beloved, do not be surprised at the fiery ordeals which come upon you to prove you as though something strange were happening to you. But rejoice in so far as you share in Christ's sufferings, that you may also rejoice and be glad when His glory is revealed."[12] Do not confuse suffering with punishment—if you are a Christian, you are not being punished for your sin. In the book of Hebrews it says of Jesus, "Although He was a son, He learned obedience through what He suffered"[13] and Jesus was found without sin.

    God is infinitely personal with each of us and relates with us according to His intimate knowledge of us. As we grow, we begin to experience freedom from our destructive desires and habits and the freedom to love in a healthy way. How ironic that dependence leads to freedom. How reassuring that we can count on the Holy Spirit to be our best friend in guiding us into personal intimacy with the Lord.

Chapter 6: Religious Abuse

I know there are those who look back with fondness on their childhood and would like to return to those earlier days when all seemed right in the world. Just another day, just another hour or two of innocence and the freedom it brought. While I envy such people, I am not one of them. I have tried to rewrite my past, deny it, gloss over it and pretend it didn't exist, all to no avail.

I was born into a very conservative, religious family. We resided in a small suburb called Parchment, which borders Kalamazoo, Michigan. Sunday, "The Lord's Day" as it was known to those in our church congregation, was the worst day of the week for me. Church was our home away from home. We would start with early morning service, which was followed immediately by Sunday school. These were loathsome, boring activities for me. Often I would find myself counting the rows of bricks that lined the sanctuary walls while the congregation recited the Apostle's Creed. The service—which was no service to me—droned on. Eventually time would pass and we would return home for Sunday dinner before heading back to church for evening services.

Meals were generally an unpleasant experience in our house—not because of the food, as my Mom was a great cook, but rather because of the amount of prayer and scripture reading that was mandatory. Grandpa would pray before and after each meal. Who could forget Grandpa praying? He would go on and on with his strong Dutch accent ringing in my ears. On more than one occasion, I got in trouble for making my brother laugh during these long appeals to God. I think Grandpa must have believed that the length of his prayers and the sound of his voice, distinctly deeper and more reverent when he prayed, were important to God!

There were always Bible readings after each meal throughout the week, but on Sunday everything seemed to drag on and on. We would all take turns reading the Sacred Word. I was somewhat of an embarrassment as I stumbled and stuttered through the readings, liberally sprinkled with "thees" and "thous."

Hardly any of it made sense to me and most of what I could understand I didn't like.

The God in the Bible seemed a lot like Grandpa. I remember one day when Grandpa found a nest of baby rabbits hidden in his garden. He marched directly to the garage, returned with a shovel and bludgeoned the small creatures to death so they would no longer pose a threat to his garden. This cruel action seemed like God to me: all-powerful and swift and direct in measure, especially when it came to sinners.

We weren't permitted to purchase anything from a store on The Lord's Day. A lady from our church once saw me buying ice cream on a beautiful Sunday afternoon and called my folks to report my sin. Fishing and swimming were also forbidden on Sundays. Thankfully, my Dad loosened up in later years and allowed us to watch the Detroit Lions on Sunday afternoon—that is, as long as it didn't interfere with Bible study. Bible study would, of course, mean another trip to the church. It would be years later before Grandpa owned a TV.

Sunday evening services were attended by only the most devout in our community, which I am sorry to say included me, not out of a sense of willingness but rather one of forced necessity. Many members felt their duty to God was adequately discharged by simply attending Sunday morning services. But not us! Escaping hell's fire and damnation was the foundation of our existence. We needed to appease God, who "hates" sinners. Prostitutes, homosexuals, drunkards, adulterers, fornicators, liars and thieves all had a place reserved for them in the Lake of Fire. They were doomed just as the poor little rabbits that had nested in Grandpa's garden were doomed. Godliness (which meant moral superiority in our family) was the answer to our sick and decaying world.

Ours was a world of outward perfection. Cleanliness was next to Godliness. Our house was spotless, with everything in its proper place. Our neighbors, who dared to paint their houses and mow their lawns on Sunday, were considered to be not much better off than those who drank away their pain at the local bar.

On the surface, ours was the All-American family. Yet, with all of the outward appearance of perfection, all was not well with my soul. Intense feelings of isolation and anger were growing within me. The roads we traveled that supposedly lead to the Golden Streets of Heaven were quickly crumbling. There were times, lots of times actually, when I felt totally alone. I thought there was something missing in me, some essential part of being human. I felt alienated from other people, like a member of another species. The world around me was driven by fear of a God who was terrifying to me—a God I did not want to worship. I didn't tell myself it was good that I was different from other people; on the contrary, I assumed I was bad. Isolation is hard to understand as a child. You know you are alone, but you feel you are not supposed to be. My life was devoid of meaningful love and fear stalked my waking moments. Most of all, I feared a God who wanted to punish me.

When I was 16, I remember sitting in church knowing that I would spend eternity in hell. If I knew I was a sinner, then God (Who knows everything) also knew, right? He knew my every thought and action, so who was I kidding? Even as the preacher proclaimed God's impending judgment concerning adulterers and fornicators, I could not stop myself from gazing at the organist with lust in my heart.

As a young teenager, I was already smoking behind my parents' backs, and it wouldn't be long before alcohol would become an important part of my life. By the time I was 18, I had acquired a fake driver's license to get me into nightclubs. One night, I got into a fight with a bouncer and trounced him soundly. I felt absolutely nothing—no fear, no pain, no regret. I was becoming numb to the fear and pain of isolation. The downward spiral continued and at age 19, with James Bond as my alter-ego, I dreamed of becoming a hired assassin. As desolate as it now sounds, I wanted to be able to kill another human being without feeling anything. This desperate determination took place just a few months before I met Jesus.

Chapter 7: Born Again

  Life continued for me in a disconnected and empty vacuum after graduating from high school. I had been a talented football player with mediocre grades in high school, and I squeaked into Hope College in Holland, Michigan based on my church connections. Unfortunately, Hope College held no hope for me. Although I lettered on the varsity football squad as a freshman, I seldom made it to class. The school interceded in an attempt to "save me" and made arrangements for me to room with a senior, who was supposed to get me back on track. What the administration didn't know was that my new roommate wasn't all that committed to helping me. Grand Rapids, with its good-looking girls and nightclubs, was just an hour away, and neither of us could resist temptation. We were ultimately both expelled.

  A subsequent trip to California resulted in yet another dismal failure in my already empty life. The year was 1964 and my friend, whom I called "The Greek," and I had packed my '57 Ford and headed across the country to the promised land of sunshine, endless beaches, bronzed surfers, and the "cutest girls in the world," as the Golden State was described so vividly in the popular songs of the day. The Greek was running away from a felony charge and one of the girls I was dating was naively planning our engagement party. It was clearly time to get out of Michigan. Instead of finding the promised land, I found that jobs were scarce, money was tight, the cost of living was sky high, and surfing was not my sport. A few months after arriving in California, I left my car with The Greek and hitched rides back to Kalamazoo. The Golden State turned out to be not so golden after all.

  I was now going on 20 and working as a janitor in a factory near Kalamazoo. Truth be told, the janitor job wasn't all that bad. I came in at noon and got off at eight, which made for a great nightlife. The work was easy and I made several friends. One guy in particular, Roger, befriended me. He was a "born again"

Christian. He didn't come on strong, but there were those little things, subtle innuendoes, which revealed his faith. Roger said I needed Jesus. He and a friend of his named Walt extended numerous invitations to get together with me. I resisted for quite some time, but I eventually accepted an invitation, never planning to keep the engagement. I tried to back out at the last minute, but in his kind and gentle way Roger said, "But my wife baked a pie just for you." *"What the hell,"* I thought, *"I'll go spend a little time and leave as soon as possible."*

That evening Roger, his friend Walt, and I sat talking into the night. I smoked one Camel after another. Back in 1964, "real men" smoked Camels. My speech was peppered with curses. Walt was doing most of the talking, and I was becoming more and more agitated. I was dead set against the conversation we were having and was sorry that I had come. How had I allowed myself to get into this fix?

Suddenly there was a moment when their words faded away and it was as if Roger and Walt weren't even there. I was ushered into another place. I had heard other conversion stories over the years, but I didn't believe they were real and I certainly knew it would never happen to me. For a brief period of time—exactly how long I can't say—my eyes were opened and I got my first glimpse of God's Glory. There was an infusion of truth, and God was there in the truth; or rather, He *was* The Truth. In that moment, I simply knew the reality that life without God was death. I also knew immediately that the story of Jesus as the Savior was not an obscure notion, but an undeniable absolute.

I had crossed an invisible threshold and my will to resist completely evaporated. Shortly after this experience I asked Jesus to come into my life. *I was born again and for the first time in my life I experienced true joy!*

****

Although I had experienced the life-giving touch of the Holy Spirit and spent peaceful time in His healing and loving presence, I would, unfortunately, once again fall prey to the deadly bondage of religious legalism. As a child, I had no choice. As a young man, I was seduced. This second encounter with religious bondage resulted in me throwing out everything I had once embraced and believed about what it meant to be a Christian. Well, almost everything….

Chapter 8: Born into Freedom—Sold into Slavery

Friends couldn't believe what had happened to me. Randy had come to Jesus! My parents were shocked and embarrassed when a Christian radio station broadcast my story. The public revelations of my soiled and sordid lifestyle prior to accepting Christ soundly shattered the appearance of the perfect God-fearing family that was so important to my parents. What would the neighbors think?

As a new Christian on fire for the Lord, I wanted to win the world for Christ. I had seen the light and was determined to convert everyone around me. As a young zealot, I started witnessing to everyone I knew. When I ran out of ammunition, I would ask Walt to intercede. Walt had become my mentor, as he was a "big gun" in Christian apologetics (defense of the Gospel). It would not be many years before I too would become one of the top apologists in town.

Although the Holy Spirit now dwelled within me and I had a burning desire to convert those around me, I was still basically me. I liked to smoke and drink, and I enjoyed being around pretty women. At the time, I didn't think of my lifestyle as being one of temptation and sin, and I felt loved by God. I soon got the message, however, from the Christian community that Christians are supposed to conform their lives to the teachings of the Bible. Reading and studying the Bible were absolute necessities. Memorizing it was even better. And the Bible had a lot to say about the behaviors and lifestyle I embraced.

After dutifully immersing myself in the words of the Bible and listening to the counsel of some of the Christians around me, I concluded that I needed to make some changes in my behavior in order to please God. I determined that some of the women I had dated were "worldly"—too worldly for a Christian—so I started dating some *good* girls from my church. These were the kind of girls you could be comfortable bringing home to meet the family. This made a lot of people happy because respectability was very important in our Christian community. I quickly discovered, however, that we *all* are basically the same—the flesh is the flesh, no matter how we try to dress it up. It is a point not worth discussing in further detail here, except to note the lesson in hypocrisy.

In 1965, I responded to the call for patriotic duty by enlisting with the Marines. In typical fashion, I wanted to outperform the best and was ultimately awarded the dress blues for being first in my unit at Marine Corps Boot Camp in San Diego. After completing Boot Camp, I found myself in Vietnam, a young and enthusiastic soldier fighting for God and Country. Top Gun! Secretly, the "John Wayne" image burned within me. I was a patriot through and through. However, by the time my tour of duty was over and I had reached the rank of Sergeant, I knew that the principles I was fighting for were misguided notions, if not outright lies. All the patriotic hype concerning God and country, stopping communist aggression, and preserving democracy quickly gave way to the ugly realities of war.

Men were laid out on the ground as one would lay out game after a hunting trip. The tortured wailing of Vietnamese women and children mourning their dead resounded throughout the land. American boys were packed in body bags and sent home after playing their parts in the theater of patriotic honor. To this day, when I hear the beating of helicopter blades, I am reminded of the senseless death and destruction I saw all around me.

In a war zone, most cultural restraints vanish as the horrifying realities of war take their toll on a person. Moral platitudes and religious beliefs that had been built on a foundation of sand crumble quickly in such desperate and ugly circumstances. An individual's true nature comes to the forefront when there is no room for pretense. Men grab for what little pleasure they can find. Make no mistake, at our core, separated from God, we are all capable of acting like animals—or should I say, worse than animals. I witnessed many men reduced to their most undignified and fallen state.

It is important to note that in the midst of this destruction and chaos, which forever changed my view of national pride and politics, I was acutely aware of God's grace sustaining me. I did not fall prey to the depravity that was the fate of so many young men. In fact, I regained a measure of peace and joy that had begun eroding in my quest for righteousness back at home. I remember being thankful for finding candles so I could read my Bible on those dark nights while hunkered down in the desert. A fellow soldier and I would cheerfully walk long distances to find water so we could fashion a makeshift shower and experience the pleasure of washing and shaving. I shared my faith with other soldiers in the presence of the Holy Spirit.

As a marine, I longed to give my all to the "cause." I volunteered to be placed on the front lines of the battle, but I was blocked at every turn in spite of my efforts to be in the thick of things. In fact, I was removed from direct battle and placed out of harm's way. I was given a coveted position in the military hierarchy and was stationed in a nice hotel. I continued to ask for reassignment to the battlefront, to no avail. Apparently, God had other plans for me.

After being discharged from the Marines in 1967, my next "tour of duty" was to reunite with the Christian organization that had discipled me in Michigan. I left Camp Pendleton and headed to Fort Worth, Texas, where Walt now lived. I adopted the organization's mission to disciple the world for Christ, primarily through building ministries on college campuses. Like the Marines, this organization meant business. They wanted the young, zealous, and idealistic to carry their message. This organization, like the Marines, was "looking for a few good men." As with many organizations that evaluate their members using quantitative standards of performance, an attitude of superiority was pervasive in the hierarchy. The measuring sticks used in this organization included Bible study, scripture memorization and recitation, as well as evangelism. Most of the Christian community was viewed as lukewarm—men and women who gave lip service to God only when it was convenient or made them look more holy. Real discipleship meant total dedication and commitment.

Though the death grip of religion was pulling at me, I was not yet fully in its clutches. The reality of Jesus was still part of my life in a natural sort of way. I was married, had a new baby boy and was a full-time college student. I was working as a police officer with the Fort Worth Police Department, assigned to the evening shift in two of the hottest crime districts in the City. I saw more action in two years than many officers who patrolled more respectable parts of town saw in a lifetime—apprehending burglars, armed robbers, murderers, and drug addicts; kicking down doors and high speed car chases were all normal occurrences in my job. I saw it all and did it all. I liked the job and it fit me like a glove.

Sharing the gospel as a police officer was simply a manifestation of who I was, and the Holy Spirit was present as convicts and the down-and-out, bums and the homeless came to know Christ. But the Christian organization I was affiliated with wanted me to go into full-time "Christian service." At first I had no desire to become part of this organization's staff, though this was a coveted role sought by many. Not yet understanding the freedom that true intimacy with the Lord brings, I came to believe it had to be the will of God for me to join the ranks of the organization, since the leadership was convinced this was right for me. Ultimately, I took the plunge, quit my job, and joined the organization. That was the day I sold myself back into slavery.

Chapter 9: Looking for a Few Good Men

Denton, Texas is a college town, and though it is only 40 miles from Dallas, the atmosphere is far more slow-paced and conservative. With its giant oak trees and sturdy dwellings built in the early 1900's, one gets the feeling of going back in time when life, at least on the surface, seemed simpler.

The year was 1969. I had moved my young family from Fort Worth to a home not far from North Texas State University (today known as the University of North Texas). As the new representative for the evangelical organization I had joined, it was my job to disciple the campus and surrounding community for Christ.

In order to be a "disciple for Christ," one must first understand what was expected. There were standards to uphold if you intended to set yourself apart from most of the community and be a "man of God." Reading, memorizing and quoting scripture were mainstays of the organization and the hierarchy set the standards for diligent Bible study. A select group of individuals had determined that some 180 verses from both the Old and New Testaments should be committed to memory. The idea was that these were promises from God that a person could claim, and therefore should be memorized.

If God wanted such commitment, He was going to get it from me. Over the next couple of years, I would memorize the equivalent of 50 chapters from both the New and Old Testaments, being able to easily cite chapter and verse when the "need" arose. If faith needed an object, what better object could one have than the word of God? In addition to studying on my own, I enrolled in a seminary in Dallas that specialized in preparing men for the ministry. Biblical scholars of great repute taught there, and I was mesmerized by their knowledge.

Witnessing to the lost was an obvious component of being a disciple, but as I look back, it wasn't something that a lot of people liked to do beyond paying lip service to the idea. I noticed that the higher one climbed in the organization, the less the leaders actually got involved with the unsaved—after all, they were busy running the organization and measuring performance. That was not true of me. I wanted to save the lost, and if witnessing was what God wanted me to do, and if it was part of being a disciple, then I was determined to be the best at it. But, something in the core of my being bothered me—if you say someone is "lost," what exactly are they lost from? Are they lost because they believe or behave differently than you? Does believing or behaving the same as another make one "found," and if so, why?

Since I had spent most of my life being *wrong*, now that I was a Christian, I wanted to be *right*. More than anything, I wanted wisdom, as I believed wisdom would be the foundation that would carry me through life. At 26, and older than many of the students at NTSU, I related more personally to some of my professors than to my fellow students. The professors' world consisted of ideas and the desire to convey what they often deemed to be important, if not perfect, knowledge, and so did mine. Debate was a popular form of academic interaction, so debate them I did. The classroom soon became the arena where the battle of reasoning was waged. It was Christian ideology opposed to humanism and relativism, the hot issues of the time. A few of my professors enjoyed the process and one in particular, an agnostic, remains a friend to this day. Still, there were others who didn't enjoy being in my presence at all. They had their agenda and I had mine. At the end of most debates, however, I left my opponents tongue-tied, red-faced and frustrated. I could defend my position, and I could defend it well.

It wasn't long before my wife and I had many students hanging around our home, also wanting to be disciples for Christ. Some moved into our home for training, and the ministry grew. We had a sense of destiny and purpose, as we were winning the world for God. I didn't realize at the time that the core of what the organization stood for, and what I had bought into, was based on the same lie that I had vehemently rejected so many years ago. As a child, the lie was manifest in the need to be "good," resulting in fear and shame. The lie was now manifest in performance. I had come full circle; once again trying to appease a demanding God.

In my personal life, I began experiencing a numbing emptiness and lack of fulfillment, although I would not (could not) admit it. God demanded sacrifice, so who was I to grumble? My marriage was a source of pain, frustration and unmet needs and desires, but divorce was simply not an option. The Bible is clear about divorce. The same was true with the lack of fulfillment in other areas of my life, but there was no way out and no way to anesthetize the pain. Drinking was not an option. Smoking was not an option. Neither was fantasy, masturbation or pornography. Unmet needs loomed and grew. So did my sense of despair, as I felt trapped by the long list of biblical imperatives. Denial became a way of life. I later learned that the main problem with denial is that you store what is denied in your basement as a kitten, but when it breaks out of the cellar (and it *will* break out), it's a roaring lion. At any rate, the only way I could make my faith work was to deny my needs and the desires of my heart. Visions of grandiosity helped ease the pain a bit. After all, I was saving the world for God, which served to feed my sense of self-righteousness. Feeling right led to feeling virtuous, which my flesh enjoyed.

Crowning one's self with virtue places one, at least in one's own mind, in the highest state of existence. The setup was ideal: Being a disciple for Christ was a lofty position and maintaining my wisdom and virtuousness seemed of great value at the time. It made the pain worth it—or at least that was the concept I embraced. I was unable to look down the road toward possible consequences. I wasn't aware that my so-called virtue was hollow and meaningless and that my pain was meant to be a warning. Not only was I was blind to what constitutes real virtue, but my understanding of faith also didn't allow for human frailty. I was caught in a death grip between my belief that I had to perform for God—the belief that God *requires* this of us—and my fleshly embracing of self-righteousness.

There were those who fit especially well within the organization, and some have remained with it to this day. Not long ago I met with a man who is still with the organization. This man became a Christian when we were in Vietnam together, almost 40 years ago. He joined me in Denton after being discharged from the military and married a woman who had lived in our home for "training." For more than 20 years, my friend headed up the organization's ministry in Mexico, and he is now back in the States with a lofty title connected to his name. We spent a couple of hours together and as we talked, he confessed that he longed for some reality in his life. He recalled the way God had touched him in Vietnam, but over the years that reality had been reduced to a vague memory. Basically, he felt alone, sterile, and not at all sure about his future. I asked him if he felt loved by anyone in the organization or in his ministry, and his answer was no. He truly felt love from no one. No one!

This is so tragic when you think about it. The only reason I, or my tormented friend, had become a Christian so many years ago was that the loving, gracious Spirit of God revealed Himself to us. He opened our eyes and our hearts. There was absolutely nothing we had to do to be *saved* except receive what Jesus had done for us. Jesus died and rose again for us. The work was done. It was complete! It cannot be improved upon. There was nothing we had to do to get "right" with God, as we were made "right" by the righteousness of Jesus.

But religion had taken hold of both of us—religion, with its formulas and rules for behavior. Religion puts us in bondage and kills the spirit of life. In religion, one seeks to please God in order to either escape His wrath or win His love, because in religion, it is never finished. Our debt is either never paid or must be repaid by proving our devotion to Jesus for having paid the debt. We lose sight of the God who truly loves us—we can't see Him in the midst of all of our activity of appeasing and pleasing.

Keep in mind that many of the activities I was involved in were *not* innocent. I am not saying that nothing good came out of those endeavors. The dorms and homes surrounding the campus held growing groups of people who diligently explored their Bibles. A great deal of time and thought went into studying God's word and meditating on His will. People came to know Christ, and healing and personal growth did occur, but it had little to do with the goals of the organization. The good that came about had everything to do with the Holy Spirit of God being in intimate relationship with individual people. For the most part, I was not performing these activities because of the leading of the Holy Spirit in my life. I was trying to win God's approval through my performance—forever pushing in order to please God. Scripture memorization, Bible study, seminary classes, prayer meetings, seminars, witnessing, tithing well beyond the "mandatory" 10%. All of these practices were strictly adhered to so that God would be pleased and I would gain special favor with Him. At the time it seemed so right. *Dead right!*

Chapter 10: My Eternal Break with Religion

My second child was born on September 10, 1970. I was the proud father of a nine-pound baby boy! Nathan Randall was his name. He was a beautiful little guy with a quiet disposition. Though there was much lacking in my marriage, there was no lack of love concerning my children. On October 13, just a little over a month from the date of his birth, Nathan Randall died. They called it Crib Death. I was absolutely devastated. "The Lord gives and the Lord takes away. Blessed be the name of the Lord," was all I could hang on to at the time, but my thoughts tortured me. It would be many years later before I would finally come to terms with his death.

"Why did God allow my son to die?" I asked myself a thousand times. Was He testing me? Did God take my son because of some sin in my life? Was God punishing me? What about all those Bible verses I had memorized, claimed and believed? I had prayed daily for my children's safety. Was my faith not strong enough? After all, the Bible says that if I were to have faith the size of a grain of mustard seed, I could move mountains.

I remembered riding home from church as a small boy in the back of my father's car after misbehaving in church. Dad stopped at an abandoned, scary-looking house and told me he was going to leave me there if I wasn't good. Was that what God was doing to me now—punishing me for not being good? Where had I fallen short? Was He turning away? Wasn't I good enough for God to protect me and that which I valued most in life? Was He testing my faith as Job was tested in the Bible?

I did the only thing I knew to do—I became further entrenched in the performance of my faith. Once again, performance had its "benefits." The higher ups noticed and started discussing my future. A power struggle ensued within the organization, and I became the focal point. Two leaders were involved in a clash of opinions concerning my career path and where I would best serve their agenda. My popularity with the discipled community in Denton had become an issue in their eyes. Power and ambition were at stake with these men. I was asked to relocate my ministry to a different city, but with the responsibilities of a growing family (I now had three young children), I did not want to move. Bucking the system resulted in a huge backlash, as submission to authority became the issue. I was emotionally hanging on by my fingernails, and the ministry I had helped develop in Denton was being torn to shreds. But, I believed God was going to work things out. I had to believe this, as the issue of my faith—my belief system—was on the line. As things grew worse, I became more desperate.

I called a well-known religious leader and told him my story. I felt trapped by my faith. I wanted out, but believed I couldn't let God down in this test of faith.

"Get out," the religious leader said to me. "None of us can live this life of faith."

"If none of us can live it," I replied in return, "why do we preach as though we do live it?"

He had no answer for this.

I called another religious leader I knew; a man who has written books on how to live the Christian life. He traveled, spoke in many Christian circles and was a gifted teacher. He listened carefully as we spoke at length. He correctly understood that I was standing on faith as we both believed it. However, it was my life that was on the line, not his. He assured me that I was doing the right thing by devoting all to God, regardless of the pain I felt. "Hang in there," he encouraged me, "God will deliver you."

Time passed and my circumstances went from bad to worse. I spent weeks staring into the fireplace, waiting for God's deliverance. Unbeknownst to anyone, I seriously contemplated suicide. I was living in silence and isolation and I wasn't going to last much longer. One particular evening, I went to bed in a fit of depression. Around two o'clock in the morning, God awakened me. Then He spoke to me in actual words that were heard by my spirit.

"Randy, I know and appreciate what you are trying to do, but it has already been done through my Son."

His words were gentle and loving and although the words were few, the understanding and illumination that went through me magnified those words a million times over. Everything to which I had devoted myself, my entire belief system, my sense of virtue and my hope for deliverance had been based on my own understanding of God's truth. My hard work and sacrifice had been in vain—I had been *completely* wrong in my understanding of the Christian life. Other than the issue of my salvation, I had forfeited the true Christian life of trust, love, hope and joy that the Holy Spirit brings for the bondage and death of religion.

For the first few days I was stunned and in a state of shock. I walked away from the ministry and took a menial job as a painter's helper. Can you imagine what that was like for a high performer like me? Going to bed believing you are another Moses or some great prophet—certainly one of the most righteous men alive—and waking up as a painter's helper? As I thought about all of the sacrifice and wasted years, a rage burned within me. I was determined to make up for lost time.

Chapter 11: Broken in the Wilderness

Wasted! Fourteen years of my life wasted! That's how I felt after the Lord showed up and "delivered" me from the hell in which I had been living. Perhaps I should have felt a measure of thankfulness, but I did not understand at the time God's gentle love and concern for me. So, I turned my anger against God. It took many years in the wilderness, alone with God, isolated from the input of others, for me to begin to understand who God really is.

I remember jogging around White Rock Lake in Dallas when the shock from God's revelation was beginning to wear off. Although I now had a respectable position working for an insurance company, I felt lost and alone. I didn't know how to deal with my anger, which was overwhelming at times, and I blamed God. "*I will never speak to Him again,*" I determined as I picked up my pace. However, it's a long way around the lake and I grew tired of muttering to myself. I turned on God and let him have it with both barrels. I raged at Him with every form of profanity my mind could muster, and I can be very profane if I choose to be. To my surprise, no lightning struck from Heaven and I felt much better as my anger subsided.

I also loathed the Bible at this point in my life. The very same Book that the Holy Spirit used to encourage me and give me hope in Vietnam, Satan had used as an instrument of death against me in the guise of seemingly righteous and religious activity. When I found myself around religious people, I became aggressive and profane. Digging myself out of the hole created by my years of false beliefs and religious bondage was not easy. I wasn't sure who the enemy was or where to find the answers. I started reading books by Leo Buscalia, Scott Peck and many others, searching for answers and meaning—searching for me.

I divorced my wife of 15 years, desperately needing to escape the pain and emotional harm that had been created by so many years in a bad relationship—a relationship that had been void of love and tenderness, yet was bound by duty, law and an angry God who didn't allow for divorce. I poured myself into my boys and my fitness routine, racing motorcycles with my two sons who had moved in with me and taking up kickboxing—the perfect outlet for my hostility. I began living for my own pleasure. I bought a new bass boat, fished whenever the urge struck, built my dream home, drove a new BMW and chased women. I started smoking and drinking again, enjoying the freedom of having no rules. I was going to grab for life wherever I could find it.

  The scandal and gossip directed my way by the religious community was relentless. It was a feeding frenzy of religious delight. People are fascinated by the demise of others—the fig leaf being torn away for all to see. I was beyond caring.

  As the years drifted by, I truly did not know what I believed. I still knew that Jesus had died for me, but beyond that my concept of God had been shattered. Prior to God's revelation, when He awakened me in the middle of the night, I spent most of my time trying to please a God whom I was *sure* I knew. I now spent most of my time fighting a god who wasn't really God at all. Satan had succeeded in deceiving me again! I gave myself over to the pleasures of this world, but there was an emptiness at the core of my being. Fishing was one of the few activities I could truly enjoy. I felt a measure of peace and satisfaction when I was alone on the lake, immersed in the challenge of catching large bass and surrounded by natural beauty. My day-to-day life was focused on working to pay the bills of my yuppie lifestyle, yet my life was void of contentment. Every goal, every relationship just turned out to be another dead end. I was a driven man, yet I was driving on empty.

  I know now that I really did not have a basis for being angry with God. After all, it was God who showed up and delivered me. But, I had so many misconceptions about who He was, and I had a lot of unlearning and relearning to do.

Broken

Watching the Olympic games invariably brings tears to my eyes. Something about the human spirit giving everything it has makes me weep. My own personal hope for glory—to be "God's man"—had turned out to be a disaster. And I had given it everything I had.

I now turned to a different pursuit of glory—one that would please and glorify me. I spent six long years writing my first novel. It was a major ordeal bringing it to completion. Writing a novel is like running a marathon. For many miles there is no end in sight. The time finally comes when you think you are near the end of the race, yet a monstrous hill looms up before you. When faced with the challenges of publishing and marketing a book, you realize you've only just begun.

My hopes and dreams came to a crashing halt about three years after my work was in print. I clearly remember one Saturday morning when the final distribution deal fell through. What seemed like a sure thing fell apart before my eyes in a way as unexplainable as the ticket agents in Kauai refusing to sell me a ticket. By then, most of my business interests were depleted and I was deeply in debt, as I had totally focused on the promotion of my book. Where do you go after giving everything you have to yet another dream that fails? I felt stripped and gutted. I had stumbled and fallen—the race was over. I was forced to declare personal bankruptcy. The humiliation of this act was unbearable, but fitting—I was bankrupt in every area of my life. The emotional bankruptcy was the most difficult, however, as I came to believe that life was not worth living. I regretted the day I was born. I became absorbed in self-pity and self-loathing; drinking heavily and spending most of my time watching movies via VCR—anything to check out. I wanted no part of reality.

Friends and family fled from me. Others gloated at my demise. This was particularly difficult for me, as I viewed many of these people as close personal friends. But I had not yet reached bottom. The bottom came when I became very ill. "Chronic fatigue syndrome" some doctors called it. I was so sick that I wanted to die and nearly did. Just getting out of bed was an ordeal. I felt like a man with leprosy who had been exiled to perish alone. My health, my dreams, and my trusted friends were all gone.

I was placed on a highly restricted diet in order to rebuild my immune system. I couldn't smoke or drink. I had nightmares through the night, and I would awake to the void that my life had become. I had been stripped of everything I valued. Who was I, now that I couldn't perform? How could I find the strength to face such total and complete failure? The disgrace, loneliness, and emptiness were devastating.

Finding God in the Wilderness

Slowly I began to regain my health—baby steps of improvement at first, then larger ones. It was progress. It was hope. I still couldn't perform physically as I used to, but my view of the world was changing. I discovered an inner peace that I had never known. The fear that stalked me for most of my life was dying. I was learning to let go and live one day at a time. My values were changing and my old way of life now looked insane to me. As the months drifted by, I gained strength in every way. I found a new sense of myself and I no longer felt alone. I was no longer defined by what others thought of me or what they thought was best for me. As a matter of fact, I became my own best friend. I was learning to love and accept myself for who I was, not who I was supposed to be.

During that period of time, I took a teaching job in east Texas at a school of last resort for troubled youths. I moved to Lake Fork and lived in a modest house trailer with no phone. I enjoyed the solitude and spent a lot of time with just the Lord. I fished and worked, and the Lord became my new best friend. These were healing years in my life. I loved being alone because I wasn't, in fact, alone. I was being transformed from death to life.

Chapter 12: Resurrection

I know what it means to come back from the dead. From a place of no hope and despair—regretting the day I was born—to a place of joy, excitement, peace, and contentment. It often leaves me feeling disoriented, as I know my part in the resurrection process has been insignificant compared to God's hand on me. Yes, I made choices. Yes, I saw God as the authority in my life. Yet, these choices and the act of submission do little to explain the abundant blessings God has bestowed on me simply because He loves me.

How does one go from being a tormented man who was never satisfied—always viewing the glass as half-empty (in reality, it probably *was* half-empty given the "non-god" I had been serving)—to one who can proclaim, "My cup runneth over?"[14] How is one transformed from a place of anger and despair to, "Surely goodness and mercy shall follow me all the days of my life?"[15] There is a newness inside of me that mystifies me and defies logic, so let's start with the more easily described, but no less miraculous, outside transformation and see where it leads.

Miraculous Transformation—A View from the Outside

Some miraculous aspects of my life are listed below in no particular order:

♥ I am now 60 years old. I like working out and staying fit. I have made the choice to stay fit, yet I have a resurrected spirit in this aging body after experiencing a total loss of physical health in my 40's. Today, there are few men 20 or 30 years younger who can stay up with me in the gym. I am thankful for my renewed health; however, I hate getting older and I'm going to fight it every step of the way until God gives me a new and glorified body.

♥ Five years ago, I was living in a house trailer in east Texas, with most of my assets depleted. My personal dreams for success and recognition had been shattered and I had endured the humiliation of declaring personal bankruptcy. A well-to-do non-Christian friend of mine asked me what I was going to do—how I was going to survive. This individual, who has no children, began planning for his retirement in his 20's, making frugal and wise investments with his savings. Although we are the same age, he was already retired at the time and enjoyed a very comfortable lifestyle. I told him I was going to keep working and follow the Lord's guidance. Today, I have a thriving and successful business that I truly enjoy. My net worth exceeds all expectations I had for myself and has me shaking my head in wonder. I could retire today, but I would be bored, so I am waiting on the Lord to show me what He would have me do with my time and resources. I am not claiming God will always—or even usually, as I can't know the mind of God—bless our choice to work hard with financial success. I can only claim He has blessed me.

♥ After experiencing a second divorce in my 50's, I am now married to a beautiful woman with whom I enjoy a wonderful relationship. We experience life-giving intimacy on every level. We have chosen to make God the authority in our marriage, just as He is the authority for us individually. The Lord has used my wife and our relationship to bring about fulfillment and joy in ways I never considered important. Among other things, my wife introduced me to SCUBA diving during a trip to the Virgin Islands and I quickly became certified. She also happens to be a gourmet cook. We enjoy eating and entertaining at home every bit as much as at the many fine restaurants we frequent in Dallas when the mood strikes us. We have a

number of good relationships that are fun, intimate, and important to us as a couple and individually. The joy and contentment with our physical relationship exceeds my wildest fantasies. Yet sex has its "proper" place in our relationship, meaning there is much more to our relationship than the sex. (I *never* thought I would be saying this, as sex was *all* I thought about at one time in my life!) Although we do not always see eye-to-eye, we submit to God in prayer and He always answers us, strengthening our marriage with each bump in the road. Before meeting my wife, I did not believe the type of relationship we have was possible. Yet I've come to believe there really is such a thing as God's perfect choice for you.

♥ I have a true sense of family and home for the first time in my life. I have come to think of my two stepchildren as my own, and I truly love spending time with my in-laws (yes, I actually *choose* to stay in the same house with them when we visit). I have a renewed and healthy relationship with my mother and siblings, after years of dysfunctional interaction. I now celebrate the fact that my brother is my best friend. My wife also loves my family and they delight in her. Our home is located in an upscale area of Dallas with manicured lawns and lush landscaping. Although it is a beautiful home, it is the feeling of being blessed within its walls that most grips me.

♥ I have learned to graciously accept and enjoy the outward pleasures in life—those things that are just plain fun. While I have learned not to feel guilty about these external blessings, I am deeply aware of the fact that all I have comes from the Lord. For example, you know how some men are about their cars—well, I get around town in a great sports car that's really fast and I absolutely delight in driving it. Or take my wardrobe—I'm really a jeans and t-shirt kind of guy in my heart, but my wife enjoys buying me clothes. She is very fashion conscious and claims that certain clothes were "made for me." I have to admit, she does know how to dress me up and I am pleased with the results. Another example is the delight I have experienced on vacations and the delight I feel when we return home. We have traveled to some of the world's most beautiful places and are purposefully finding more time in our schedules to enjoy more frequent vacations. But, I still love our home. For me, no other place can compare to the comfort of being in our home, as home is truly where my heart is. Even hobbies have taken on a new meaning for me—the Lord has given me a renewed spirit for fishing. I recently purchased a beautiful (my wife would question the use of this adjective) new bass boat with all the latest electronics. My wife has commented that I have enough tackle to open a retail store. Although that's an exaggeration, I must admit I have a lot of great tackle and I love "playing" with it. In the past, fishing represented a necessary escape from the pain and disappointment of the world. Fishing now encompasses everything I desire a hobby to be—relaxing, enjoyable, challenging and perfect for me. The true delight of it is that the Lord still fishes with me!

I make choices to include God in the pleasures of my life and He accepts my invitations. How remarkable!

Miraculous Transformation—A Changed Heart

Though I am deeply grateful for the abundant outward blessings the Lord has bestowed on me, it is my relationship with Him that truly sustains me. All the toys and trappings in this world are meaningless to me apart from Him. As I mentioned earlier, most of my life was spent peddling into a 50 mile-an-hour head wind. Now I have that wind at my back. How can this be? How can one truly change from the inside out? The Lord also sustains my relationships with others and gives me the ability to extend myself in love—something of which I am incapable apart from Him.

I'll now attempt to explore the transformation of my heart, which, I might add, is at the heart of the sanctification process:

- ♥ Perhaps one of the biggest transformations is in the area of my sexuality. For example, how can I love *only* my wife and want *nobody* else? From our first date to the present, I have not fantasized about another woman. How can this be? Much of my life was built on fantasy. After chucking religion for good, I began subscribing to *Playboy* magazine. The problem was that I found I was never content in any of the relationships I formed, finding the fantasy better than the reality. Before *Playboy*, when I was in bondage to my religious beliefs, denial and law were a way of life. The lack of fulfillment and emptiness at that time were even worse. None of my sexual or emotional needs were being met, but I had no choices under the do's and don'ts of religion. Divorce wasn't an option, fantasy wasn't an option, seeking pleasure outside of the marriage wasn't an option, unclean thoughts weren't an option and admitting failure wasn't an option (as this would imply that God had failed me). The list went on and on. Only sacrifice, obedience and self-denial were options. As the years of unmet needs passed, I feared Satan had the edge over God when it came to pleasure, but a part of me knew this couldn't be true. Thankfully, I have found that God's plan not only meets my needs, it blesses me with the desires of my heart.
- ♥ The intimate physical and emotional relationship I have with my wife is unbelievable because it comes from the Lord. The fact that I want absolutely nothing to do with pornography and I don't fantasize about other women is certainly not who I am in the flesh, but it is who I am in Christ. That's not to say I don't find other women attractive, because I do. In fact, I've never found women more attractive than I do today. However, I know there's only one woman for me, and she happens to be God's choice for me. When temptation comes at me, I simply say,

"Lord, this is not for me—I don't want it, take it away!" My needs are met by the woman I love and I can enjoy relationships with other women without desiring them sexually. I love the personal freedom I have with my transformed heart, yet it still seems like a miracle to me as the transformation has occurred in the context of grace. God has simply written His law on my heart.

♥ Relationships outside of my marriage are also miraculously different for me today. I often used to relate to many people in ways that weren't healthy for me—either needing their approval or relating out of guilt or a sense of rescuing them. Now I don't need or expect people to sustain me at my core, as God does this for me. I also know I cannot rescue another person. Ironically, this lack of dependency on others has allowed me to extend myself, resulting in loving, life-giving relationships. No human being has any control over me, as living my life before God has set me free. True independence and freedom come only through a dependent relationship with God.

♥ I love my work and I wonder how this can be. I have always worked hard, but when I was in the ministry, I turned my back on money and pleasure. After my break with religion, the size of my paycheck became my focus. Money was a symbol of freedom that allowed me to do whatever I wanted, whenever I wanted. The actual work itself was burdensome to me. Winning the lottery would have been a dream come true. I can tell you now that this is no way to live your life, as it is really not living at all. I am well suited to my profession, and God has given me special skills that allow me to excel at what I do. I delight in helping my clients, I delight in being challenged, I delight in making a sale and I delight in the financial reward of my work. God created us to delight in our work and to find fulfillment in a job well done. Simply amazing!

♥ One of the greatest changes I have noticed is that there is no place I would rather be than where I am right now. You see, I never used to live in the moment. I was always looking down the road toward some goal I had not yet achieved, looking for better times than the present. For years, I needed alcohol to give me any sense of well-being, and I was never content. I was always moving in a new direction—anything to avoid the emptiness of the moment. It was like some unknown force was chasing me. It's not that I'm an idle person now because I am usually on the move, but I am now infused with a sense of well-being which only God can give. I can stop and enjoy the life God created for me. I know that tomorrow will take care of itself, so I waste little time fretting about it. I don't have a clue what the future holds for me, but I know the One who's holding it. And He loves me.

****

I could go on and on about the miraculous changes that have taken place at the core of my being, but I hope you get the picture. Jesus said, "I have come that you might have life, and have it abundantly."[16] I know what that means for me, and I know many of you have discovered what it means for you as well. But what about those of you who don't yet know what it means? ***To possess that real and abundant life Jesus promises—where do I begin?***

Chapter 13: The Choice

It took many years for me to understand what constitutes real faith and the abundant life we are promised if we choose to be intimate with God. I have come to know that real faith has very little to do with what we call knowledge. Rather, faith is about a relationship of trust with the God who absolutely loves us. Faith is also about choice—the choice of responding to the Holy Spirit who helps us grow in our faith. Unfortunately, many people who call themselves Christians have substituted their belief system—their knowledge—for faith and an intimate, trusting relationship with God. The trouble is that our belief systems have their sources in us and are filtered through our fallen nature. Our fallen nature is what is referred to as our "flesh," which is the part of the human spirit that is in rebellion against God. Real faith, on the other hand, rests in the very character and Person of God. The personal "I Am," the One who created us in His image, can and does deliver us and give us abundant life if we truly come to know Him and surrender to Him.

At first this statement sounds like really good news. In fact, it's the best news you are ever going to hear, but it is a good news, bad news sort of thing. The bad news is that it is impossible to live the Christian life apart from the life-giving power of the Holy Spirit. And although God created us to be intimately connected to Him, He does not force Himself upon us. We have to choose! He grants us true freedom, which is amazing when you consider His power.

Satan, on the other hand, is very forceful and is a skilled liar. Evil comes at us with the idea that true freedom is being independent from God. Of course, to one degree or another, we have all bought into "the Lie." And in our desire to be lords of our universe, we find ourselves in bondage. We cannot find lasting meaning, purpose, joy and life on our own, independent from God. Our flesh doesn't like that. The flesh is the flesh and it does not change. Try as we might, we cannot patch it up or put on our Sunday best to dress it up. The flesh has to die. That's the bad news part about being a Christian.

The good news, however, includes the defeat of Satan. ***If you are a Christian, Satan has absolutely no authority or power over you.*** As a matter of fact, *you* have authority over Satan. Although this is true, Satan constantly comes at us with lies—appealing to our flesh that exists in opposition to the leading of the Holy Spirit. But, and this is a very important but, evil *cannot* gain control over you or me unless we submit to Satan's lies. We have power over those lies, but we must choose to submit to the Holy Spirit. Often you will find that the right choice—the choice put forth by the Holy Spirit - is the most difficult one.

For example, how many husbands and wives are, at this very moment, experiencing difficulty in their marriages? I venture to guess that the number is staggering and the sources of the difficulties run the gamut. Maybe the passion has gone out of the relationship. Maybe there's no intimacy. Maybe there are serious disagreements over money, children, aging parents, politics, priorities, and so forth. Needs are not being met, emotions are running high, weariness or apathy has set in and neither person knows where to turn. We are often willing to spend hundreds, if not thousands, of dollars for counseling when the answers we seek are so often readily available to us if we are simply willing to turn to the Lord to guide us in sorting things out. This is not to say that the Holy Spirit will not lead us into counseling, rather the point is that the direction comes from the Holy Spirit rather than from our own quest for solutions. Often we are willing to do anything but get down on our knees in submission to the Lord. I believe pride and an independent mindset keep us from experiencing the grace of God more than any other tactics we employ.

Keep in mind that it can be very easy to miss the leading of the Holy Spirit in our lives because the Lord will not shout or bully us in any way. He won't pressure us to come to Him. He usually speaks in a quiet and gentle voice—a voice that is easy to miss. And with God, there is always complete freedom to say no. We have to choose to submit ourselves to His leading, and often His purposes stand in opposition to our beliefs and the systems that control this world.

It is ironic that God's ways often don't make sense to us, but religion, with its rules, fear and punishment does. Like it or not, we are involved in spiritual warfare and Satan wears many hats that cater to our flesh. Satan knows our fallen nature and frequently comes to us disguised as an angel of light. He is also a master at quoting scripture. Making the Bible an absolute truth—the infallible "Word of God"—apart from the leading of the Holy Spirit is one of the biggest lies and most effective tools of bondage Satan has used against the Christian community since the crusades or the fall of mankind. The Holy Spirit may lead you to study the Bible to witness the historical working of God in the lives of people. From Genesis to Revelation, there is knowledge to be gained. However, anything you find in the Bible is simply a part of the menu. The meal is the reality of your personal relationship with God—the actual dynamic of the resurrection. Demons know that Jesus is resurrected and that He is the Lord of the universe and will return. To study the menu and refuse the meal is death. Jesus addressed this very issue with the religious leaders of His day when He said, "You search the scriptures because you think that in them you have eternal life: and it is they that bear witness to me. Yet you refuse to come to me that you might have life."[17] **Jesus is the Word of God!** How easy it is to miss this truth in our quest for knowledge.

When you think about it, the religious mindset and the desire to be lords of the universe are pretty much one and the same—different sides of the same coin. Both are separated from God and function independently. The religious bring sacrifices of their own doing and give them to gods that they have created in their own image. This will always lead to either guilt—I should be doing much more for God, wretched person that I am—or self-righteousness. The more we bring, the better we feel about ourselves. This is especially true if we cling to our belief systems, while adding a healthy dose of personal sacrifice. Either way, we don't deal directly or intimately with the Lord.

In the exercise of real faith, you have nothing to stand on but the Lord Himself—you are fully naked before Him. There's nothing in our lives that we can't bring before God, as He already knows what troubles us and what satisfies and delights us. Perhaps you are lonely and want to be in a relationship. Perhaps you are having problems at work. Maybe you are out of work. You may have a destructive habit in your life. We live in a world of addictions and twisted motivations. Food, drugs, alcohol, pornography, religion, money, power, work, self-image, and a host of other things bombard our senses and battle for prominent places in our lives. Our flesh wants instant gratification and fulfillment. But, God will meet you where you are and deliver you if you really want to be free. The same power that raised Jesus from the dead resides in us in the Person of the Holy Spirit.

Although this miraculous, restorative power resides in us, real faith also understands that we cannot manipulate God into doing for us what *we* want Him to do. We are in control of nothing as it relates to God and what constitutes real and resurrected life. I frequently have conversations with God where He seems to ignore my specific requests. For example, He seldom delivers me from my circumstances. However, the specific requests of mine that God always answers are these: *"Take away my fears, Lord"* and *"Let me see this situation through your eyes."* He changes the way I view my problems. As the fear abates, I realize there is nothing lacking in my life. Either I discover that I already have what I desire and need, or I simply must go out and get it with His blessings (He seldom drops in my lap the desires of my heart without me putting forth some measure of effort). Fear is connected to separation, loneliness, emptiness, need and death. When fear doesn't exist, I know that I lack for nothing. The beauty in surrendering to God is that when we get to know Him He takes away our fears. "There is no fear in love because perfect love casts out fear."[18]

We talk about God being a loving God, but do we really believe it? I have witnessed the deep and abiding love of God, not only in my own life, but also in dramatic ways in the lives of others. One particular experience comes to mind that I believe reveals the true nature of God in a profound way that erases all doubt. Years ago, while I was praying with a friend, I was aware that the Holy Spirit had fallen over her. I did not move or say anything. Soon, I noticed tears streaming down her face. At first, I found this confusing, as there is no fear when communing with the Holy Spirit. All I could do was wait. After a period of time, she revealed what had transpired. In those brief moments, my friend saw herself as a lamb held in the arms of the Shepherd. She was being cradled in the lap of God. With certainty, she knew she was completely loved. She was loved simply for who she is—loved just for being. When she felt the tears spilling down her cheeks, she wanted to stop them and said so to the Shepard. It was then she realized the tears were not her own. The tears streaming from her eyes came from the Lord. They were God's tears. God felt her pain. He infinitely felt her pain more than she. God was crying for her.

    It can be a scary thing to surrender your mind and heart to the living God, as you have to establish this relationship for yourself. Getting naked before Him is not all that easy. No fig leaves—nothing to hide behind and no one to hold your hand. The preacher or priest won't be there. Neither will mom or dad, brother or sister, husband or wife, friend or support group—no one will be there but you and Him. But Jesus gave us the assurance we need to surrender when He said, "Come to me all of you who labor and are heavy laden and I will give you rest."[19] It is between you and the One who created you. One day, each one of us will independently come face-to-face with the God of the universe—the Great I Am. This is the same God who, at the Second Coming, will destroy Satan and all satanic power with the word of His mouth. True freedom, joy, unimaginable energy, and lasting glory lies only in the capable hands of God. We only have to choose.

****

    The other night, I was wrestling with the Lord over this manuscript. *"Why can't I find the right words?"* I asked Him.

"Why can't I connect the dots? I'm being transformed from death to life and, try as I might, I can not connect the dots." I was frustrated and wondered if finishing this manuscript was even worth trying. *"If I can't connect the dots for myself, I certainly can't connect them for others,"* I was telling Him. Several minutes passed and then the Lord answered me in His gentle sort of way: "***Only I can do it***," He said.

Am I slow or what? This has been very hard for me to get—only God can do it. Only God can connect the dots for you and me. Maybe I can be a part of the process, helping to point you in the right direction. Maybe I can warn you about the pitfalls I have encountered. But, only the Holy Spirit can enlighten you.

Each one of us must work out our own salvation, which requires the on-going choice of surrendering to the leading of the Holy Spirit—the choice to know God intimately. Although I am very slow, God is very patient and very loving and I am finally coming to understand my choices. I now have begun to see what Jesus meant when He said, "I have come that you might have life and have it more abundantly."[20] And I also know what David meant when he said, "Surely goodness and mercy will follow me all the days of my life, and I will dwell in the House of the Lord forever."[21] It really is nice having the wind at your back and knowing that you are completely loved. Jesus loves me and I love Him in return. Simply amazing!

END NOTES

1. Matthew 23:28 r.s.v.
2. John 16:7 r.s.v.
3. John 14:26 r.s.v.
4. Romans 8:1 r.s.v.
5. Acts 9:5 r.s.v.
6. 1 Corinthians 15:9 r.s.v.
7. Ephesians 3:8 r.s.v.
8. 1 Timothy 1:15 r.s.v.
9. Genesis 3:5 r.s.v.
10. Genesis 3:7-10 r.s.v.
11. Psalm 46:10 r.s.v.
12. 1Peter 4:12-13, r.s.v.
13. Hebrews 5:8, r.s.v.
14. Psalm 23:5 r.s.v.
15. Psalm 23:6 r.s.v.
16. John 10:10 r.s.v.
17. John 5:39 r.s.v.

18. 1John 4:18 r.s.v.

19. Matthew 11:28 r.s.v.

20. John 10:10 r.s.v.

21. Psalm 23:6 r.s.v.